AND I DIDN'T EVEN SHOOT
Memoirs of a Postmaster

Written by Tanya E. York

Illustrated by Joseph Chang
(Grandson)

Cover by Jaci Leigh McKim

AND I DIDN'T EVEN SHOOT
Memoirs of a Postmaster
©2008 by Tanya E. York

All rights reserved under the International and Pan-American Copyright Conventions. Printed in the United States of America. No part of this book may be reproduced or transmitted in any form, by any means, without written permission from the author.

Published by Tanya E. York
P.O. Box 141
Depoe Bay OR 97341-0141

Manufactured in the United States of America by Newport LAZERQUICK in conjunction with Dancing Moon Press.

Book Design: Kathleen Keck
Cover Concept: Talley Woodmark
Cover Design & Photo: Jaci Leigh McKim
Illustrated by: Joseph Chang

ISBN 978-1-892076-49-6

Library of Congress Control Number 2008907255

York, Tanya E.
And I Didn't Even Shoot - Memoirs of a Postmaster
1. Title
2. Northwest Author
3. Depoe Bay Oregon
4. Memoirs
5. Post Office

First Edition
August 2008

I would like to dedicate this book to the following people:

First of all … my mom .. who challenged me to always believe I could be a success at whatever I attempted.

I want to thank my children, Lisa Rhinehart, Monica Bryant, Billy Summarell, Clint Summarell, Perry York, Jr., and my wonderful grandchildren and great grandchildren. You are my greatest blessings.

I want to thank my dear friend Talley Woodmark. When I was so frustrated trying to come up with an idea for the book cover, there she was with a wonderful concept. She put me in touch with the right person and wa-la, the perfect cover.

And last, but not least, my best friend … my husband Perry for always being there for me and believing in me. I love you.

I love you all
Tanya

PREFACE

This isn't a novel, or even an actual story as one might expect it to be. It's just some of my thoughts and observations over the years as a postal employee. I'd like to thank the co-workers, managers, customers and most of all .. my family. You have inspired and encouraged me throughout my career. You will all live in my memory and my heart forever.

Lovingly
Tanya York

A MOTHER'S CHALLENGE

I can still remember the phone call to Mom that would forever change my future. I had called her to chat, and during our conversation I said, "I sure wish I wasn't so old (I was in my forties) so I could get some schooling and have a career with a good future, benefits, and even a retirement." She said that I had once remarked how I'd like to work for the Post Office, so why not contact them and see what I had to do to get employment.

We talked awhile longer, and before we ended our call, Mom said, "Honey, don't put this off. Call tomorrow morning and get the ball rolling." I promised her I would.

The next day I had a real hectic morning and kind of forgot about my promise to call about the postal exam until that afternoon. You know how it is when you promise your mom you'll do something. It will haunt you until you do it.

Anyway, I was living in Prineville, Oregon, so I called the local Post Office. I was told I had to call the Bend, Oregon Post Office as that's where the exams were taken. I was told the Post Office was doing exams the following day but there wouldn't be enough time to get the info to me and get me signed up for the exam. I asked what the worst case scenario would be if I came to take the exam without any studying and failed. Could I take the exam at a later date? How long would I have to wait? Anyway, every reason I was given, I politely argued that I'd still like the opportunity to take the exam the next day. Finally, I was told to be at the exam site half an hour early to fill out the necessary paperwork. I think they just wanted to shut me up and thought, oh, well, why not humor her.

So there I was, shaking like a leaf and wondering why on earth I had promised my mom I'd do this. All sorts of thoughts were going through my mind. Would I even be able to answer one question? The sum total of what I knew about the Post Office was … you put the correct amount of postage on your letter or package and away they go to their destinations. Was I ever in for a surprise!

The people at the exam site were so kind and eager to put everyone at ease. They had been in our shoes themselves and knew we were nervous. They were very professional, yet very kind and understanding.

The exam was nothing like what I expected. There was mathematics, reading comprehension, memory exercises, etc. At the end of the exam, I came away feeling good about everything but still nervous about what my score might be.

When I finally received my test score and discovered I'd passed, I could hardly wait to call Mom and let her know. She was just so calm. "I knew you'd do it," she said.

THE INTERVIEW

I guess I sort of expected to receive a call any day to start work with the Postal Service. After all, I had passed the exam.

I was soon to discover that's not exactly the way things happen with the Postal Service. You see, it's not just a job. Working for the Postal Service is a very desirable career and you have to wait until either someone retires, someone gains upward mobility into a management position, or someone transfers to another office creating a vacancy. You then receive an interview (which many other hopefuls also receive notices).

Well, just as I was about to think I'd never get considered for employment, I received my long-awaited-for notice of an interview for possible employment at the Prineville, Oregon Post Office. Oh, how I prayed to be hired. I had lived in Prineville many years, so it would be perfect.

I thought I'd been nervous about taking the exam and anxious when waiting for notification of an interview. Well, let me tell you … I was so scared and nervous about the upcoming interview. It was sort of like first date jitters, taking your driver's test with someone other than a parent beside you in the car, and diving off the high diving board into the pool for the first time all rolled into one. What should I wear? I wanted to look professional enough that the interviewer would think I'd represent the Postal Service in a positive manner. Don't wear anything too loud. They'll think you're a hussy. Don't wear anything too dull. They'll think you're a meek little nobody who won't exert themselves and be a good employee. Don't wear this. Don't wear that. I'll bet I tried everything in my wardrobe on at least a few times.

The day of my interview finally came, and I know I must have been visibly shaking as I walked into the Postmaster's office. I wasn't going to let him know just how scared I was, so I just thrust out my hand to shake hands with him and announced, "Hello. I'm Tanya and I'm here for my interview."

Bill Layton was the Postmaster at the time and he returned my handshake with a firm handshake and a friendly, "Hi. Come on in and have a seat." I guess I hadn't fooled him about my nervousness because he started the interview by asking me about myself and my family to put me at ease.

We then talked about the Postal Service and why I wanted to work for such an organization. I was honest with him and told him because I was a good, hard worker and I wanted a career, not just a job. I said I thought the Postal Service could provide that for me and I, in return, could do a very good job for the Postal Service.

Then he really threw me when he asked me what my postal career goals were. I was so surprised by his question that I just blurted out what I'd been thinking since the moment I'd started the interview. I said, "I don't just want to be a worker my entire career. Someday, I want to be sitting where you're sitting ... a Postmaster ... representing the Postal Service." I was thinking to myself, 'I hope I can someday sit across the desk from someone and inspire them to strive to become a Postmaster because they see in me a true love of what I do and pride in the organization I work for the way Mr. Layton has inspired me today.' At that moment, I knew I wanted to work for the Postal Service for the rest of my working years. I prayed I'd get the opportunity.

I left that interview with a real war going on inside myself. Would I get hired? What if I didn't? Oh, how I wanted this job! I would work so hard to prove to Mr. Layton that he'd made a good choice in hiring me.

The Interview

JUST PART OF THE CREW

I was nervous as I was invited, once again, into Mr. Layton's office. I only prayed he had asked me to come because he had decided to hire me and not to tell me he had decided to hire someone else. He shook hands and then got right to the point. "Well, Tanya, how would you like to come meet the rest of the crew?"

Had I just heard right? Had Mr. Layton just told me he was hiring me as a Letter Carrier? This was too good to be true. If I'm dreaming, don't let me wake up, I prayed.

"Tanya, I'm hiring you as a PTF Clerk instead of a Carrier. I just found out I need a Clerk and I think you'll do a good job," Mr. Layton said.

I wasn't sure what PTF meant, but I didn't care. I was going to work for the Postal Service. I answered that I'd try to do a good job at whatever I was hired to do.

It's a wonder I didn't fall over my own feet because I was walking so high off the ground I couldn't feel if I even had feet as I followed Mr. Layton to meet the rest of the crew. He said to call him Bill because he was one of the crew. He said he just wore a different hat than we did.

That one statement probably impacted me more over the next twenty years than any other one statement I'd hear. It taught me that a really good manager leads their crew by example, not by leading with an iron fist. I learned from Bill to never ask your employees to perform a task that you aren't willing to get in and do yourself. I'm so grateful to have started my postal career under such a great example of leadership. He always cheered each employee on in their endeavors.

Don't get me wrong. Bill was very exact in what his expectations were. He set a very straightforward, positive example of a postal employee, and he expected the same from all of us. He expected us to do our job the very best we could.

That didn't mean he expected exactly the same amount of production out of each employee. If you were simply "keeping up" with someone else but were capable of exceeding that, he'd expect you to do so. He expected us to continually challenge ourselves. He'd say to not worry about challenging the other person, to just always challenge yourself and you'd continue to grow. I've tried to carry that philosophy into other aspects of my life, and you know what? It works. So started my career as a postal worker.

A BIGGER BRAIN PLEASE

It didn't take me long to realize just how much there was to learn about this organization I'd come to be a part of. I thought I'd never be able to learn even part of what everyone else around me seemed to know. I did learn that a PTF Clerk means Part Time Flexible Clerk. That means my schedule wasn't always the same. It varied as to what the office needs were.

I never knew there were so many different ways to mail a letter, let alone a package. My goodness! All those forms! I'd never be able to know one from the other. You know what though? It's like learning to crawl … then walk … and before you know it, you've learned to run. The funny part is, you can't remember when you went from crawling to running. It just seemed to happen.

One of the first tasks to tackle was learning the "office scheme". That didn't mean I had to learn how to be scheming (thank goodness). It meant I needed to learn which addresses went to which carrier. When I was handed these pages and pages of streets and addresses, I thought, 'You've got to be kidding. I'll never be able to learn all of this.' That first day of my "address challenge" was something else for sure, but I was determined to figure it out somehow.

That night I called Mom and told her how worried I was. Her answer was to go about it another way. She reminded me how I was always good at remembering stories, so maybe if I could relate each address for a particular route to a story, it would help.

The next day I was eager to try this new approach. I made up these silly stories for each route's addresses. The street names weren't so bad. The real challenge was the weird breaks in the numbers. 301 Fir Street through 368 Fir Street and 380 Fir Street through 399 Fir Street might go to City Carrier 3, while

369 Fir Street might go to City Carrier 1 because of where the house sits on the block.

Just when I was thinking, 'Yeah! I'm finally on top of this address stuff,' because I'd actually been able to learn the entire address scheme, I'd get a new challenge. Here we go again, old girl. Oh well. Challenges keep you young (I think).

A Bigger Brain Please

THE MISSING WORDS

As my postal education continued, I would discover you don't use words for a lot of stuff. There's lots and lots of numbers and acronyms though. Just ask any Clerk that works the window line, sorts mail, processes claims, processes incoming bulk mail, returns or forwards mail for a variety of reasons, and they will tell you there are form numbers for EVERYTHING you do.

A notepad is either a "buck sheet" or a "Form 13" depending on who you're talking to. You don't have just daily financial paperwork to turn in from working the window line, you have a PS Form 1412. If you have a very laid back day (there aren't many of those), you might have to only deal with the following PS Forms: 1000, 1091, 1093, 1500, 3501, 3502, 3544, 3546, 3547, 3575, 3800, 3811, 3817, 8105, 8125, 3083, 3806, plus EP9, Lab 152. I'm sure I've overlooked some we use every day, but these are a few.

Of course, there are those abbreviations we live with. You postal workers will know the ones I mean ... like DMM, IMM, DOIs, DALs, CASS, OCR, BMEU, COD, CMRA, ASC, 204B, MPOO, IRT, PVI, just to mention a very few.

I challenge anyone not employed by the Postal Service to follow a postal worker around for just one week and I can guarantee you will come away with a greater respect for what it takes to be a postal worker. I don't know of any time in my life when I've worked with such hard-working and dedicated people. It's the largest "family" you'll ever belong to and they will always be there for you.

A TEAM MAKING MEMORIES

Each year there was always a Christmas parade in Prineville. There were floats, bands, marchers, and especially that wonderful gentleman, Santa Claus. It was something young and old alike looked forward to each December. Folks would stand along the parade route, in the snow, waiting for the magical wonder of the decorated floats. The local organizations, churches, and businesses would work their hearts out to design the winning float.

That first fall after I went to work for the Postal Service, I asked the Postmaster if we were going to enter a float in the Christmas parade since the theme that year was "Christmas Around The World" and that's what we did ... deliver Christmas around the world. He said he had no problem with us doing that if we could get enough employees to participate on their own time.

Well, we did. In fact, every last employee volunteered. There were City Carriers, Highway Contract Carriers, Clerks, Supervisor, and Postmaster all working side-by-side. We all worked our behinds off getting that float ready. We laughed and joked, and when the day of the parade came, we were all so proud of what we'd accomplished as a team.

We dressed the children, grandchildren, nieces and nephews of the employees in costumes from countries all over the world. Many long hours were spent by the employees and their family members making the intricate costumes to be worn by those sweet children. It was so touching to see those children from two years of age through twelve years of age as they proudly sat and stood on that float representing the children from all over the world. Their faces glowed with excitement and pride as they took their places on that flatbed hay trailer pulled by one of the employee's pickup truck.

There were four adults on the float to make sure the children were safe. I was so proud when I was asked to sit in a rocking chair with some of the smaller children sitting in front of me. I was dressed as an old granny with white hair and glasses, and I was to be reading a Christmas story to the children. (I wouldn't need a wig now ... it would be natural.)

We had decorated two City delivery vehicles to be driven by City Carriers. One of them was just in front of the float and one right behind the float. The employees had gotten together and purchased some candy which the children on the float and the Carriers in the delivery vehicles threw to the crowd.

The Postal Service won Grand Champion for our entry. The Postmaster proudly hung that ribbon in our lobby for everyone to see. I can still see all those employees and our Postmaster on our hands and knees making all those posters about how the Postal Service delivers Christmas around the world every year. I'm sure each and every one of those employees involved still smile about that wonderful time we had and what a show of teamwork there was.

I think that's why I've always loved the Christmas season the very best while working for the Postal Service. Because no matter how tired and stressed you may get, just let someone come to pick up a package, and their face lights up when it's a package from a family member or friend, and it's all worth it. You suddenly forget the tiredness and the racing the clock to get everything done. You just smile to yourself and say a little prayer of thanks for being put in a job where you can bring so much happiness to so many.

And you know what? It's not just at Christmas ... it's all year long. Postal employees get the joy of seeing someone's face light up when they receive those pictures of a new baby in the family, a birthday card from family or friends, or best of all, when someone gets a package or card for no reason other than someone thought of them. Postal workers are the most blessed group of working people because they get to be a part of bringing that joy into someone's life. How exciting to be part of such a TEAM!!!

A MONSTER ROLLS AMONG US

Not too long after I began my postal career, a new employee was hired. One morning I was carrying a tray of mail from the letter sorting case towards the box section to be placed into the P.O. boxes. I heard the Postmaster yell to the new employee to "stop and pull back hard" as he also grabbed for the handrail and pulled with all his might. The employee had come from the back dock pushing a BMC (Bulk Mail Container) fully loaded with parcels and weighing hundreds of pounds onto the workroom floor without first checking to make certain the path was clear. I looked over my shoulder just in time to see this monster piece of equipment coming towards me.

I held tight to the tray of mail in my arms and jumped aside to avoid becoming a grease spot on the floor. I almost made it too! The equipment caught my left heel. It was so fast that I didn't even know for sure if I'd actually gotten struck. My foot felt numb, so I thought I'd lucked out on that one.

Bill (P.M.) was there in a flash and asked if I was okay. I said I thought I was. Then I took a step and Bill noticed there was blood everyplace I stepped. He had someone take the tray of mail (I didn't drop any) and he got a chair for me to sit on so he could check my foot. With rubber gloves on, he gently lifted the bottom of my pant leg and announced he would be taking me to the doctor. After checking the injured foot, the doctor announced my Achilles tendon had been badly torn. I'd be stitched, bandaged, and in a walking cast for awhile.

My biggest concern wasn't for my foot. I was hoping this wouldn't affect my future with the Postal Service. Bill assured me everything would be okay. There were many new things he wanted me to learn and this was the perfect opportunity.

The P.M.'s philosophy was for every employee to know every task in the office. That way, if there was an emergency, there would always be someone to take over and the office would continue to run smoothly. I'd come to appreciate that train of thought and put it into practice when I became a P.M. years later.

During my rebound from my combat session with the BMC (which I lost), it was decided I would become knowledgeable in the administrative part of the Post Office, such as doing the daily books. I was anxious to show my talents as I had always excelled in all mathematics.

It didn't take more than a couple of seconds for me to get all prideful notions of my abilities right out of my head. Talk about feeling dumb. With a lot of patience from the P.M. and a bottle or two of aspirin (he actually ended up still having his full head of hair), I finally learned the administrative part of running a postal facility.

Over the years, I'd come to know that a manager must also be a babysitter at times, a mediator, have a memory like an elephant, be able to do twenty things at once while planning ahead for what needed to be done several hours or even days down the road, know the employees and exactly what their production capabilities are so at any given time, under any circumstances, they know who to put where so things run smoothly. A good manager must not be afraid to take a firm stand, yet have a true caring for the employees and be able to balance the two.

I also learned a manager's true merits show in how well they prepare their employees for upward mobility by the way they constantly encourage them to challenge themselves. Never compare one employee to another's capabilities. This will discourage the one to not try and give false pride to the other. Instead, encourage both to continually challenge themselves and you end up with both employees being successful and your job is made easier. Everyone wins.

A Monster Rolls Among Us

EXILED TO THE MIDDLE OF NOWHERE

"Tanya, can you come in here a minute, please," the Postmaster called one morning. Oh, Lord! What had I done wrong? I swallowed hard and went to face my fate.

As I entered the office, the Postmaster asked me to take a seat. Wow! This must be bad. Then he said, "I have an assignment I'd like you to undertake, Tanya. I received a call from headquarters stating there's a need for an OIC (Officer in Charge) for the Brothers, Oregon Post Office. I was asked if I had an employee to send, and I thought you could do the job fine. You're doing a good job with the books. You're doing good at the window with customers. Do you think this is something you'd like to tackle? It would mean a round trip each day of 104 miles."

I thought if he had confidence in my ability to undertake this challenge, then I was game. I guess this would show if all the time and patience the Postmaster had given to prepare me to stand up to the challenges I may face in the future years was well spent. Let's see. I'd need to gather up all of my notes and segregate them so I'd have "cheat sheets" to help me if I needed them. Thank goodness I hadn't thrown them out. (At least I didn't think I did.) I kept telling myself it would be okay.

Heck! I didn't even know where Brothers, Oregon was, but I was always too stupid to know there might be something I couldn't do, so I said, 'Sure. If you think I can handle it, I'll give it a go." I asked the P.M. for directions to get there.

That day, when I ended my shift at work, I decided to go for a little drive and see just what I'd let myself in for. After an hour and twenty minutes of driving, most of which entailed driving over a dusty, graveled road, I arrived at this town they call Brothers, Oregon. I took one look and knew God sure had a good sense of humor. The only thing I saw was a store with gas pumps out front and a few buildings kitty corner across the street with a sign stating they belonged to the Oregon Highway Department.

I parked my car and went into the store to ask directions to the Post Office (which I was certain I'd somehow passed). The lady behind the counter was very kind and pointed over in the corner. She said no one was there though because he'd already left for the day.

Oh, my! What have I gotten myself into? I just knew that I must have screwed up so bad that the Postal Service wanted to hide me out here in the middle of nowhere. Well, I'd show them! I'd be the best darn OIC they could want … well, at least an okay one.

The next day at work, the P.M. assured me he was only a phone call away if I needed help. He then went over, again, the things we had gone over the day before regarding my schedule and said I'd be starting the next week. The assignment was to be for a short time. I guess a short time in postal terms isn't the same as in mine because it lasted several months.

I'm so thankful I had that opportunity open up for me so early in my career. I learned so much … like how to really think things through when faced with a challenge, and sometimes how to show patience with yourself. That's a hard thing to learn sometimes. It's easier to show patience with others than with yourself.

I met some amazing people while at Brothers. There was the weathered old rancher who drove over 15 miles that first day just to welcome me aboard. Here he had a ranch to take care of and yet he took the time out of his busy schedule to put a newcomer at ease. The wife of one of the employees of the Highway Department brought me a bouquet of flowers from her garden so I'd have something bright and cheery for my "office".

Probably the most memorable person though was the little boy who came in each day with his mother to get their mail. He was five years old and very shy. Each day I'd say, "Hi," and ask him if he was having a good time. He'd just huddle close to his mother and shyly say, "Yes, ma'am."

I'd asked the Postmaster from Prineville if I could take a few of the postal coloring books to give to some of the children, and he said, "Sure." The next time my shy little friend came in, I gave him a coloring book. You'd have thought I'd given him a great treasure. From that day on, we were fast friends. I discovered he was a real little jabberwalkie. He nearly talked my ear off from that day on.

One day he brought me a small, flat rock. He'd painted it with his poster paints. He said it was a present to sit on my desk. I thanked him, and each day he'd check to see if my rock was still there. When he saw it was still there, I'd get this wonderful (front teeth missing) smile that just melted my heart.

To this day, whenever we drive through Brothers, Oregon on our way to Idaho or Nevada, I always remember that precious child and those wonderful people who showed so much kindness and patience to this newcomer.

HEY! THAT'S NOT A DOG!

The Postmaster called me into the office one morning and said he needed me to carry mail on the Auxiliary City Route. I'd lived in Prineville for several years and knew the area which this would encompass. I thought, 'Okay. How hard can that be? Piece of cake.'

Well, I came back to the office that day with a whole new respect for Mail Carriers. They must be the smartest people in the world to remember where each and every mailbox is located. They also have to be the bravest people on earth.

On that first day as a "Mail Carrier", I had a run-in with a big yellow cat. As I walked down the sidewalk, I approached this property that had a wooden fence surrounding it. On the inside railing of this fence sat this beautiful yellow striped cat. The cat sort of swiped its paw at me as I walked past, but I thought it was just being playful.

The mailbox for that address was mounted on the fence near the front gate. As I got closer to the mailbox, I noticed the cat had followed me. 'Oh, how cute,' I thought. 'He thinks I came to see him and wants to play.' WRONG!! This cat tried to claw me every time I tried to place the mail in the mailbox. I'm thinking, 'Yeah. Right. You always hear stories about how dogs and mail carriers don't get along and here I am probably the only mail carrier in the history of the Postal Service who comes into contact with an attack cat.' I was about to admit defeat and take the mail back to the office (I could just hear the Carriers laughing), when the cat must have decided I wasn't much fun because he left and I was able to deliver the mail and continue on.

It's good though to get out of the office and get to know the postal customers. It gives you the opportunity to help them with their vocabulary challenges. You will get this opportunity especially if you are a new Carrier around the third of the month and you don't have their mail delivered by the same time as their "regular" Carrier does. They will go out of their way to share with you all the new words they have learned. They will even share with you how they can put some of those words into sentences. Yes, it's very educational being a postal employee. I would learn, over the years, that this knowledge is not for Carriers alone. Clerks are also given the opportunity by customers to enhance their knowledge of our language.

Hey! That's Not a Dog!

A WHITE-FACED CARRIER

Another call into the Postmaster's office ... this is getting to be a common occurrence. It seemed the Postmaster at the Powell Butte, Oregon Post Office was going on vacation for two weeks and my Postmaster wanted to send me to fill in. I told him I'd love to have the chance to do that. Powell Butte is a tiny little town nestled in the wheat and potato fields between Prineville and Redmond in central Oregon, and I was anxious to have the opportunity to work in a small, easy-going office.

The next two days, I spent time with the Powell Butte Postmaster so he could issue me stamp stock to last the two weeks and show me what I'd be expected to do during his absence. I was looking forward to this new challenge.

Powell Butte had one Rural Carrier and a couple hundred P.O. boxes. The Carrier was really nice and a very hard worker. I was settling in very nicely, enjoying the opportunity of meeting the local customers and thanking my lucky stars for this wonderful career I'd been given.

I shouldn't have been so laid back, I guess. For anyone not familiar with central Oregon, it's high desert country with lots of rocky terrain. It's very cold in the winter and very hot and dry in the summer. Powell Butte is mostly ranches. There are lots of "critters" living in and around the area. There are those four-legged kind and then there are those no-legged kind. I'm talking about the kind that wiggle and rattle across the ground. Those are definitely not my kind of critter.

As I found out, they apparently weren't the kind that appealed to the Rural Carrier either. One day she came into the office after delivering her route and looked visibly shaken. I asked her if she was okay. I thought maybe the heat had gotten to her. She then shared her story with me.

She was almost finished with her route when she pulled up to the mailbox in front of a ranch and prepared to put the mail into the box. She opened the box and nearly fainted. There, staring at her, was a coiled-up rattlesnake. After she had treaded air for a good six feet, she realized the snake was dead. Someone had deliberately put that snake in the mailbox all coiled up like it was ready to strike. They had propped the head up with a small stick.

The rancher whose mailbox the snake was in had two young boys about twelve and fourteen years old. I thought they may have been the culprits, so I stopped at the ranch on my way home that night. I knocked at the door, and when a gentleman answered the door, I introduced myself and explained what had happened. He called the boys onto the porch and asked them if they knew anything about someone finding a snake in the mailbox. Both boys turned beet red and said the snake was dead and wouldn't hurt anyone. They said they were just joking.

I explained to the boys the seriousness of their prank and told them delivery of their mail could be stopped for such things. And besides, what if that carrier had suffered a heart attack? How would they have felt when they had to explain to her family that they were only joking?

I wouldn't be surprised if those two boys were escorted to the woodshed by their father that night. I know he marched them into the Post Office that next morning and made them apologize to the Carrier. Somehow I think that was an end to their pranks for awhile. At least there were not anymore critters of any kind in the mailboxes that I know of.

A White Faced Carrier

McMINNVILLE, OREGON

Daddy passed away the year after I went to work for the Postal Service. All of my brothers and sisters (there were ten of us) still had children at home. My children were all grown, and since I was alone too, Mom and I spent most of my vacation times traveling together.

Mom was the greatest traveling companion. She had a sense of humor and we laughed and joked a lot. Raising so many of us kids, she could never afford either the time or the money to go to places like Reno, Nevada. I used to get so tickled at her. She was so lucky. I remember her getting my sister Teri Lynn and I going to play Bingo whenever I'd go for a visit. We got more enjoyment out of Mom's excitement than actually playing the game.

My next vacation was coming up and we planned to go to Reno and then on down Highway 395 to Oceanside, California where my sister Frankie and her husband Randy lived. Mom had been asking me for awhile to check about a transfer closer to her, so we talked and decided to forgo Reno on this trip and return early so I could check with some of the nearby Post Offices regarding a transfer.

The day after returning to Mom's, she drove me to the Post Offices in Amity, Sheridan, Willamina, Lafayette, Carlton, and Dayton. I talked to Postmasters at each office only to find they had no openings but would keep me in mind if any openings came up.

I was getting pretty discouraged. We'd planned to check with the McMinnville Post Office last. My brother Pat and his wife Sarah lived there, and we'd planned to see them after we were finished. I didn't hold much hope, but to make Mom happy, I pretended I was excited.

I went in and found the Postmaster wasn't there. The Clerk Supervisor was there however and I was shown into his office. I was told a position might be coming open soon and if I'd leave my name and some qualifications, they'd see if they could use me. I was afraid to get too excited after so many times of being told there were no openings. I just figured the supervisor was being nice to me and that I'd probably never hear from either him or the Postmaster.

When I got into the car, Mom asked what had transpired. I told her the supervisor had said an opening may be coming up in the future. I said that I didn't know how far in the future, but Mom, being the optimist she was, said she knew I'd get the transfer soon. I think at that point she already had me living in Sheridan and was planning our future trips to Reno. I was wishing I had her optimistic outlook on things. All we could do was wait.

Sunday, I returned home to Prineville, not really expecting to hear anything from any of the offices for awhile. I planned to tell the Postmaster as soon as I got to work Monday what my plans were just so he'd be prepared if any of the offices contacted him down the road.

Well, as luck would have it, I didn't have to tell the Postmaster. As soon as I arrived Monday morning, Bill called me into his office and said he'd just gotten off the phone with the supervisor at the McMinnville Post Office asking for my OPF (Official Personnel File). There go those acronyms again. It seems they were considering me for a transfer.

Boy! Was I ever caught by surprise! I sure didn't expect to hear anything yet. Bill was very encouraging and said if they wanted me he'd agree, but he'd need time to replace. At this point, I still hadn't met the Postmaster at the McMinnville PO.

The following week, I found I'd be transferring to McMinnville. They had agreed to wait a couple of months while Bill hired and trained someone to replace me. I guess Mom's optimism had paid off.

THE BIG MOVE

One morning I was informed I'd be starting work at the McMinnville Post Office in six weeks. I could hardly wait to call Mom with the news. Then the reality hit me. Oh my! I had to sell my home, pack all my belongings, rent a storage unit in McMinnville until I found a place to buy, work every day, and figure out some way to actually get my belongings from Prineville to McMinnville. I had to accomplish all of this in a mere six weeks. Could I do this? Well, like I said, I was always too stupid to know I couldn't do something, so here goes.

That evening, I was mowing my lawn after work. My neighbors came over to chat a moment. They were commenting on how they loved my place with all the trees and the wonderful array of flowers. I had an acre at the end of a lane and it was real peaceful there. My neighbors said if I ever decided to sell, they would like first chance as that would give them two acres. I told them it was funny they should mention my selling because I was transferring to another Post Office and was, indeed, going to sell. They asked what price I'd be selling for. I mentioned a price, and they said that sounded like a fair price. They went home, and I finished mowing my yard.

As I was putting the lawnmower into the tool shed, my neighbors came back over and said they'd discussed it and wanted to buy my home. I explained that I still needed to live there for six weeks before I could sell. They asked if we could close sooner as they were getting ready to leave on vacation in two weeks and would be gone six to seven weeks. They said they would be willing to have a paper drawn up that would allow me to reside in the home for the time needed. I said I'd contact my lawyer the next day and have him draw up the necessary papers and set a date and time to meet and close on the sale. We shook on it and they went home happy, while I just stood there dumbfounded. Well, I'll be. Just like that I had my home sold. I guess this move was meant to be.

That night I called Mom with the news. She was all excited. She said she'd rent me a storage unit and I could pay her when I came down. Now to get down to the task of packing. (I really hate packing!)

The very next night, Mom called saying she had talked with my brother Pat and he and my brother-in-law Dale could come in two weeks to haul my household goods to the storage unit. Another obstacle was out of the way. If my luck could just hold, I'd be so thankful.

The next day at work I was telling a couple of my coworkers of my good luck so far. I said, "If I can just manage to get everything packed, I'll be tickled to death."

That evening, as I was knee deep in boxes, someone knocked at the door. When I finally stumbled and climbed my way over and around the stacks of boxes and opened the door, there stood four of my coworkers. "Hi, you guys. What's up?" I asked. They said they thought I could use a helping hand (or in this case, eight helping hands). Those wonderful four stayed late that night, plus came back two other nights, to help me finish my packing in time for my brother and brother-in-law to transport my belongings to their new destination. When I told my coworkers I'd never be able to thank them enough, they just said, "We're postal family. That's what we do."

That's so true. Just like any other family unit, we sometimes get irritated with one another, but we're always there for each other when we're needed. What a warm and wonderful feeling to be part of such a large, close-knit family. It taught me to never take those I work with for granted … to be thankful for each and every one of them (even when I may get a bit irritated with one of them). Through good times, bad times, sad times and happy times, they're family and will always be there for you. Make sure you're there for them too.

These wonderful "family members" sure pulled a fast one on me though when they found out I was transferring to the McMinnville, Oregon Post Office. It just so happened that our Postmaster Bill Layton had gotten a great promotion to Manager of Post Office Operations (MPOO to us postal workers) in Granada, Mississippi and was leaving close to the same time as I was. Some of my co-workers asked me to help them do a surprise BBQ for him and not breathe a word to him. I said I would. For a couple of weeks, whenever I'd see someone with their heads together, I thought nothing of it. I assumed they were making plans for Bill's going away shindig.

The day of the BBQ came and everyone from the office was there with their families. We all ate too much, and then it was time to present the gift to Bill that the whole crew had gotten him. Our Supervisor was going to do the honors. You should have seen the looks on both my face and Bill's face when we were both called front and center. It seems Bill had been told the BBQ was for me and had innocently helped to pull it together. Talk about a bunch of closed-mouthed people. I'd never have thought that many people could keep that big of a secret for so long. I'm amazed to this day that not one word was leaked by anyone. They were so proud of themselves.

My last day at the Prineville Post Office was both happy and sad. Even though I was looking forward to this new adventure in my life, I was sad to be leaving all the wonderful people who had become such an important part of my life.

Always remember to take time to tell those people in your life who matter to you just how much you appreciate them.

A NEW ADVENTURE AWAITS

I was nervous as I entered onto the workroom floor that first morning. I still hadn't met the Postmaster yet. What if he decided he didn't like me? Would he be sorry he'd hired me? So many thoughts were going through my mind.

Then, there was Joe, smiling and saying, "Good morning, Tanya. Come meet the crew." Everyone was so nice as they welcomed me aboard.

Man!!! I thought the Prineville office was big! The McMinnville Post Office had eleven City Routes and a lot more Rural and HCR Routes. Just like before, my first assignment was to learn the office "scheme". Joe said I was allotted 40 hours to learn the scheme and then I'd be given my test. I worried that I wouldn't be fast enough because there were so many more addresses to learn. Oh well. Here goes. I'll give it my best shot.

Joe took me to one of the letter sorting cases and handed me this tray with a large stack of addressed cards and said to let him know when I was finished. I sorted all of the cards into what I hoped was the correct slots.

I was a little nervous as I let Joe know I was finished. After he checked all of the cards to see if they were sorted correctly, he called me into his office. "Tanya, you made 100 percent. Good job. Now I expect no errors in your sorting," he jokingly said.

I'd been at McMinnville Post Office about a week and a half when I finally met the Postmaster. He'd been gone on vacation and had just returned. I only hoped Joe had given him a good report on my work. I needn't have worried. The Postmaster held out his hand to shake mine and informed me Joe had said I was a good employee.

Even in a family as close and caring as the postal family unit there are family members who go astray and have to be dealt with. One of our family members at the McMinnville Post Office broke one of the trusts bestowed upon us by our customers. It was heartbreaking to see her escorted from the premises.

Hearts were heavy in the office for several days. It sure brought home to all of us though how important it is to cherish that trust given to us and to never take advantage of that trust. We are the custodians of our customers' precious mail and should always treat it with the greatest care and protection. We can go out of our way to get a misaddressed piece of mail to someone 10,000 times and no one says a word, but let one time of something bad happening and everyone comes down on the entire Postal Service. We are a group of very dedicated people who care about our jobs and don't want to ever let our customers down.

DON'T TURN YOUR BACK ON A LOADED GPC

It was hard at first to get used to getting out of bed when some people are going to bed. Sometimes, especially during the Christmas season, we had to be at work at 3:00 a.m. in order to get all of the mail sorted and delivered on time.

I remember one morning when our Supervisor was helping to unload the GPCs (General Purpose Containers) that held stacks of magazines that had been bundled and strapped. Someone at the main office in Salem had placed some large parcels on top of the stacks of magazines. Probably wanted to save space, I guess. Anyway, during the transporting of the full equipment, the load shifted just enough to make it unbalanced. We checked the load prior to beginning to unload the GPC and felt it was okay.

The Supervisor and I had unloaded a parcel each from the GPC and I had just started to take my second parcel when the whole load shifted and that large 40-some pound box came sliding straight at me. Joe grabbed for the parcel but wasn't quick enough. The box bent me backwards and I fell in a heap to the floor.

Joe asked me if I was okay. I didn't want to be a baby so I said I'd be fine, but when I went to get up I couldn't. Joe insisted on medical attention and then called my brother to let him know what had happened. At first they were afraid I'd broken my back, but it turned out to be just a badly strained muscle. I felt like such a fool. It took awhile before I could do any heavy lifting, but I was still able to sort mail, so I guess I was of some good to the office.

JUST SPOILED BRATS

When I was asked if I would like to try my hand at the ODIS testing (Origin, Destination, Information System), I told the Supervisor that I already knew how to do that. He then showed me this laptop computer and, boy, was I at a loss as to what I should do. He just laughed and told me that this was a new, faster way of doing ODIS tests.

I struggled through the learning part and actually had a pretty good time doing the tests. What happens when doing the testing is this. You check to see what class of mail the piece is. Is it a letter, a flat, or a parcel? Does it have stamps, meter strip, imprint, etc.? Is there a legible date on the piece that indicates when it entered the mail stream? Where did the piece originate? How many days did it take to reach its destination? All of this pertinent information is fed into the computer and is used to help the Postal Service continually improve its service.

I was sent to other offices to do this "testing" on their mail. It was pretty interesting and I got to meet some pretty neat people. At least most of them were pretty neat.

One day when I was in the middle of doing an ODIS test at one of the neighboring Post Offices I heard a commotion from the workroom floor and raised voices. It seems two of the Mail Carriers were angry with each other and were ready to "get at each other" right then and there. They had to be subdued and were both reprimanded by the Postmaster. He came back to the office mumbling about dealing with "spoiled brats" and how they needed a good spanking.

I went back to my own office that day and told my Supervisor about the "spoiled brats" and he said he knew exactly how the Postmaster felt because he'd felt that way more than once. I thought to myself that I sure didn't think I wanted to be in management if it meant dealing with adults acting like children.

A VOICE FROM MY PAST

One day, while sorting letters, a name just jumped out at me. You know how it is. You're just going about doing your job and out of nowhere you see the name of a person you hadn't thought about in years. That's what happened to me.

I was raised north of Tillamook, Oregon, and when I was about six or seven years old, I had a babysitter named Carol who grew up and married a gentleman named Filkowski. Now how many Carol Filkowskis could there be in this state?

Anyway, I looked her up in the phone book, and sure enough, it was the same Carol who had paddled my behind as a child. We began to spend time together talking about all that had transpired in our lives. My mom was excited to see her after all these years too.

I, my sister Teri, and Mom would all go play Bingo every Friday or Saturday night and invited Carol to go along. It was a lot of fun to listen to Carol and Mom talk over old times, and Teri and I even got to hear some stories we hadn't heard before. Be careful how you act and what you say as a child. It may show up in the form of an old babysitter when you're least expecting it.

I'm sure I never did those things that warranted a paddling. Well, maybe just one or two. I think I do kind of remember locking my younger brothers and sisters in the closet and telling them there was a green man that was going to get them. And there was the time I talked Teri into walking along the top of the porch railing. Just because the porch was above the garage beneath our house, is that any reason to scold me? After all, I did tell her I'd catch her if she fell. Watch out for those old babysitters. They can come out of nowhere to haunt you.

IT'S GREAT TO HAVE THE LAST LAUGH

The week had been really hectic. The mail load was especially heavy all week due to the volume of cards and packages for Mother's Day. I was really looking forward to having the next two weeks off. My mom and I were looking forward to our trip to Reno and on down to southern California to visit with my sister Frankie and her husband Randy. We had a lot of fun traveling together. Mom had a sense of humor that made any trip with her a joyful memory.

She had promised my brother Pat and his wife Sarah to watch their son and daughter for them while they were out of town on a business trip. They were planning on returning on Sunday, so Mom and I were to stay Friday night and my brother Dan would come Saturday morning and stay until Pat and Sarah returned so Mom and I could get on our way, as we had reservations in Reno for Saturday and Sunday nights that had been made for a couple of months.

I got off work at two o'clock on Friday, met Mom, loaded our luggage up, and we were on our way to pick up Jamie, my niece, and head to Tim's ballgame. After the game, we bought take-out for dinner as Jamie had a babysitting job until 10:00 p.m. and Tim was having a friend stay the night.

Mom and I settled in to play Yahtzee, Scrabble, and Backgammon. We had the best time. We got to laughing over some "remember when" stuff and before we knew it, it was 11:30 p.m. We decided we'd better hit the hay as I'd promised Tim to help him roll newspapers at 5:30 a.m. and drive him to deliver the papers. When we returned, I'd call my brother to come and then fix breakfast for everyone.

We were going to use my mom's car on the trip, so after helping Tim roll all the papers, I went to let Mom know I was taking her car keys and taking Tim to deliver his newspapers.

As I walked into the bedroom, I softly said, "Mom, I'm taking the keys now."

My mom was probably the lightest sleeper I'd ever known. I swear she'd hear the flutter of a fly's wings if one flew into the room where she was sleeping and would wake up immediately. When she showed no signs of waking up, my first thought was that I shouldn't have kept her up so late the night before and that I'd let her sleep awhile. But as I turned to leave the room, something just didn't look right.

I walked over to gently touch her and realized a child's worst fears had come to be. My mom had passed away in her sleep. At first I thought, 'My God! Here I am with three kids in the house.' What to do first?

Well, I woke Jamie up and told her she needed to go downstairs immediately and keep the boys down there because I needed to do something and I'd be right down. Then I called 911. The dispatcher stayed on the phone with me until the police arrived.

As soon as they arrived, the officers were wonderful. They just took over and I went downstairs and, as gently as I could, I told the kids. I explained that I had to call their parents to come home immediately and had to call other family, so I was counting on them to be very brave for a few minutes.

I called Pat and Sarah with news I never thought I'd be having to share with them. I then called other family and went to be with the children downstairs in the family room while the officers were doing what they needed to do.

It wasn't until my sister Teri and her family arrived that it dawned on us that today was our sister Frankie's birthday. At first I thought, 'How awful for Frankie to have this happen on her birthday.' Then I thought, 'No. Frankie was the one on whose special day God has chosen to take Mom home because of the very special bond they had.' Although I had to be the one to discover our mom had died in her sleep, I'll always be thankful for those "last laughs" that we shared. It really taught me to cherish those times we have with family and friends. To always take the opportunity to laugh together. You never know when it'll be "the last laugh".

I DARE YOU, I DARE YOU

After my mom passed away, I really came to depend on the friendship that had developed with Carol, my old babysitter. On the weekends, we'd go play Bingo or go see a good movie. We'd always end up talking about how much fun we all had when Mom was still here.

On one such weekend, Carol and I had gone to Salem to play Bingo. On the way back from Salem, I told Carol I was going to play Bingo in Sheridan the next day (Sunday) and invited her to stay over and go with me. She said she'd enjoy that.

Sunday morning, we were sitting at the table having some "girlie coffee" (you know … the kind with the flavored creamer) when I heard a big thud against the front door. I went to see what had attacked my front door and found a complimentary Sunday edition of the Statesman Journal. I'd never read that particular paper before but thought, "Why not? It's free."

Anyway, we were reading different sections, and when I came across the section that had the personal ads in it, I began reading the ads to Carol, and we really had us a huge laugh over them. I jokingly said that we should place an ad. That way we wouldn't have to make a commitment because then we couldn't get hurt. We could go to dinner or a movie once in awhile yet be safe from getting "involved". I laughed, and Carol said, "I dare you. I really dare you. You don't have the guts to do such a goofy thing."

Well, saying "I dare you" to me is like waving a red flag in front of a bull. Before I could even think about it, I picked up the phone and placed an ad. It was not a very involved ad. It simply said, "Are there any decent men out there? I doubt it, but if you think you can convince me otherwise, call."

Well, by the next weekend, I was thinking that I'd lost my ever-loving mind. I'd never even considered doing something like this. What could I have been thinking?

The following Wednesday evening I was bored and thought, 'What the heck. Might as well check my messages. There probably aren't any anyway.' Well, well. Was I in for a surprise! I had nine messages. I listened to all of them and deleted all but one. There was just something about the fifth message that caught my attention. I hung up, but kept being haunted by that deep voice.

I reached for the phone about a dozen times before I finally decided to let it ring on through. A deep voice said, "Hello." I nearly hung up, but found myself telling him I was the one who placed the ad about not thinking there were any decent guys left. We talked for a few minutes and then he said he knew it probably wasn't proper, but he wanted to know if I'd give him my phone number because he really wanted to talk to me but wanted to do it on his dime. Now I have to admit that impressed me. I wasn't sure I wanted to give my number, but for some reason I found myself giving it to him.

He called back and we talked for over two hours. I found out that he lived in Depoe Bay, Oregon. He said that he was bored on that past Sunday evening and there wasn't much on TV to watch, so he was checking out the personal ads and having a good laugh. He came to my ad and didn't pay it much attention either. A few minutes later, he picked the paper up again and re-read my ad. He circled it with a yellow highlighter pen, folded the paper and set it aside. He kept glancing at it for the next couple of days and finally called on Wednesday.

Well, we talked every evening for two or three hours for over two weeks when one evening he asked if he could come see me that weekend. I thought real quick and lied through my teeth saying I was going to be in Lincoln City (a few miles to the north of Depoe Bay) on Saturday and maybe I could drive on down. I wanted our first meeting to be on his home turf, not mine, in case we didn't click.

We decided to meet at Gracie's Sea Hag (a restaurant in the center of town). Boy! Talk about being nervous. I was like a high school girl getting ready for her first date. I must have tried on every piece of clothing I owned.

Anyway, Saturday came, and when I walked into Gracie's and saw this good-looking guy turn and smile, my heart just melted. He later told me he had his life all figured out until this little bundle of fluff walked through the door and he knew he might be a goner.

We talked for a long time, and he finally asked me if I'd like to see the big town of Depoe Bay. I didn't have to tell him that Depoe Bay was one of my favorite places to come on the coast. He drove me around the town and took me down to the waterfront to show me his charter boat, the Amigo. We then drove to the wayside park at the south end of town where we sat at a picnic table and talked and watched the ocean.

Finally, the time came for me to leave because I had to work the next day. He drove me to my car and said he'd sure like to see me again. Of course I said yes.

When we really started to get serious, I put in for a transfer to the Lincoln City Post Office and was hired right away. Eight months later I became Mrs. Perry York. We didn't tell anyone when we left for Winnamucca, Nevada to get married.

After we had gotten married, we called our kids, who were thrilled and only wanted to know what took us so darn long. That was the best darn dare I ever took in my entire life. Life with Perry just keeps on getting better as the years go by. Don't be afraid to take a little dare now and then. Who knows what wonderful things might be waiting!!!!

AM I REALLY READY FOR THIS

As I entered from the back dock onto the workroom floor that first morning, it was butterflies again. My gosh! You'd think I'd get over being jittery on a first day on the job at my age. I came to find out over the years that you never get over it.

The supervisor Doug Hval introduced me to everyone, and then I was given those wonderful, much anticipated (yeah right) scheme training sheets to study. But first, it was to the box section to box thousands of pieces of mail. Not by myself though, thank goodness.

I found out that first day that one of the regular Clerks was assigned the task of handling the box section forwards and she took that job to heart. You had better not make a mistake in "her" box section or you'd hear about it for certain.

At first I was thinking she was a real bear. Then I slowly got to know her and found out she was one of the nicest, biggest hearted people I'd ever met. Just goes to show you .. don't judge someone too prematurely. They just might surprise you.

I learned the "scheme" and began to challenge myself each day to sort a little faster than I had the day before. I never challenged the other Clerks ... just myself. I knew what I'd done the day before, so I knew what my new mark was.

One day some people from headquarters came to the office and Doug called me over from the letter sorting case. He asked me to sort a tray of letters and, as I sorted, I heard him comment about how fast I was. I told him that I used to pick fern with my dad when I was younger, and me and my sister Teri and our brother Mike used to race each other and my dad to see how many bunches of fern we could pick in an hour. (There are 52 fern in each bunch that had to be tied off with fern string.) I said I guessed that's where I got so fast doing things accurately with my hands.

A few weeks after coming to the Lincoln City Post Office, the Postmaster Ralph Peterson and Doug called me into the office and asked me if I'd like to be trained as a 204B (Relief Supervisor). I said, "Sure." And so started my journey into the life of management.

Most of the time everything went okay. Every now and then though one of the crew would get a burr under their corset and give me a little grief. At first I took it personally, but I came to realize that it wasn't me, it was management in general that they had a problem with. I also learned that the ones who complained the most and the loudest were the very same ones who'd look for any reason whatsoever to drag out their time.

I didn't have much patience with the ones who felt they were entitled to drag their feet while their fellow co-workers beat feet to do a good job. I used to tell them that I'd never ask them to do anything I wasn't willing to get in and do and work my tail off to do, but I did expect them to do an honest day's work for the pay. Sometimes it was hard to be in a management position one day and then work as a Clerk beside them the next day.

When Ralph received a promotion and was sent to Eugene, Oregon, Doug applied for the Postmaster position and was promoted. I worked as 204B for a few months until a permanent Supervisor was hired.

During this time frame, I had the opportunity to fill in as Postmaster when Doug was on vacation or out of the office for any reason. Also during this time, I was lucky enough to be a part of hiring a new clerk by the name of Roberta Polly. She was a little on the slow side as far as sorting when she first started, but I was very impressed by her accuracy. I felt the speed would come later. As she progressed, I approached Doug with the idea of training her as a 204B for Saturdays and when I was on vacation or filling in for him.

Roberta turned out to be an absolute great employee that you could always count on. I'm so thankful to have had the chance to see her grow in her postal career. It was a very good opportunity for me because I finally understood what my first Postmaster meant when he said each time he saw an employee under his supervision advance it gave him a personal thrill. It was even more special when I was promoted to Postmaster in Siletz, Oregon and Roberta was appointed Supervisor when the new Supervisor was promoted. I feel so blessed to have been a part of that.

MY DAUGHTER ... MY HERO

I'd gone home for lunch that day. I normally ate lunch at the Post Office, but I had an extra long lunch break that day and thought I'd just drive home and eat.

As I walked in, I noticed there was a message on the answering machine. I listened as I heard my sister's voice asking Perry to call her, to not let me call or take any messages until she had talked to him first.

My knees went weak at the panic in her voice and I immediately called her. She asked if Perry was there with me and I said, 'No. Tell me what is wrong.' She really didn't want to tell me anything, but finally said she would on one condition ... that I'd call Perry and have him come home as soon as we finished. I promised. She told me my grandson Keith had been in a terrible car accident and had been life-flighted to Bend, Oregon. They didn't know if he was going to make it or not.

My first thought was that I needed to get to Bend and be there for my daughter Lisa. She had gone through having her oldest son Heath life-flighted to Bend when he was involved in a wreck on a three-wheeler when he was ten years old. He had a pretty rough time of it but is fine now ... all grown up and a blessing to us all.

I called Perry and told him he needed to come home immediately. Then I called the Postmaster and told him I couldn't work that afternoon and why. At first he said he needed me to work, but then realized the situation was very serious and said okay.

Perry arrived home and we called the hospital in Bend. I talked to the nurse and she couldn't and wouldn't give me any information except that I needed to get there and be there for my daughter. I think I knew then that the doctors hadn't been able to save our precious grandson. I just kept praying all the way on the drive to Bend that he'd be okay.

We walked into the hospital just as Lisa and Danny came out of the room where they had been talking to the doctor. One look at my daughter and all I could do was open my arms for her and hold her close. This was my first-born. This was the precious child who taught me how special it is to be a mom. When she was small and got hurt, I could always kiss it and make it better, but this was a hurt I couldn't kiss and make better. It broke my heart that my child was going through a pain that no parent should ever have to go through.

Her first words to me were that at least we'd had him to love for seventeen years rather than never to have known him. As I watched this brave woman, this child I'd given birth to, as she made it her goal to help Keith's friends and classmates deal with his death, my pride in her soared. She was going through the toughest pain she'd ever experienced as a mom, but she was a mom and these children, Keith's friends, were in pain and she had to comfort them. She's quite a gal, this daughter of mine.

I think back to the year before Keith died and how I had taken five of my grandchildren for the whole week of Spring Break. We had so much fun and I took a lot of pictures. I can still close my eyes and see all of them playing on the beach, looking in awe at the airplanes at the air museum in the blimp hanger in Tillamook, Oregon, laughing as we checked out everything at the Enchanted Forest in Salem, Oregon. We really built some memories that week.

Always take the time to build your own memories. You don't even need to go anywhere to do it. Just build them every day where you are.

A SURPRISE OF A LIFETIME

I remember back when I had my first interview to go to work for the United States Postal Service and I told the Postmaster that someday I wanted to be sitting where he was sitting. Well, I guess that day has finally arrived. I just got the phone call today from Jim Bogroff, the MPOO (remember?), telling me I was being promoted to Postmaster in Siletz, Oregon.

When the date was set for my swearing in ceremonies, I sent invitations to every Postmaster and Supervisor I'd ever served under, besides all my family and friends. The two wonderful Clerks at the Siletz office made sure to have posters put up for all the local customers and did one heck of a job making sure all the mail got up on time in spite of all the hullabaloo going on around them that day.

As the time for the ceremonies got closer and people started arriving, I was blown away because so many Postmasters and Supervisors were there. I couldn't help but think that it would really be perfect if only Bill Layton could be there, but Granada, Mississippi was a long way from there. Maybe he'd call and wish me luck. That would be awesome.

All of a sudden someone tapped me on the shoulder and said, "So you wanted to sit where I was sitting, huh?" I turned around and could hardly believe my eyes. There stood my first Postmaster. I nearly fell over. How could he be here? He was in Mississippi. He told me that when he found out I'd gotten that much-longed-for Postmaster position, wild horses couldn't have kept him away. He had asked Mr. Brogroff if he could say a few words, and I've never felt so humble as when this (in my eyes) "giant of a Postmaster" stood there before my customers, family, friends, and coworkers and said that hiring me had been one of the best hiring decisions he'd ever made.

I made myself a promise then and there that I would never make him sorry he'd said those words. When I found out later that he had used his vacation time and paid his plane fare out of his own pocket to come to see me sworn in as a Postmaster for the first time, I cried buckets.

When the local newspapers took photos of me with all the Postmasters and Supervisors that had come, even they could hardly believe how many were there. I'm not sure if they just wanted to make sure I wasn't after their jobs or what, but I was certainly overwhelmed by their presence.

Like I said, the Postal Service is like a big family and we all rejoice in our family members achieving their goals. If Roberta Polly ever reads this book, I plan to be at her ceremonies when she gets sworn in as a Postmaster one day. Like Bill said, wild horses couldn't keep me away.

A THREAT TAKEN SERIOUSLY

I had always worked in a larger postal facility, so there was a period of adjustment when I first got to Siletz. First of all, most of the customers were upset with me because one of the Clerks, Candy, who had been there a long time should have had the position as far as they were concerned. I knew I really had my work cut out for me if I was going to fit in with the locals.

Candy was terrific and assured them I'd do them a good job if they'd give me half a chance. She and Carolyn were top notch crew, to say the least. Those two girls could get more done on accident than most could get done on purpose. I was sure glad to have them.

I had only been in Siletz about three or four months when a young Indian girl in her late teens or early twenties came into the Post Office and wanted the mail out of a specific Post Office box. I checked and found the box had been closed for non-payment for over two months. I told the girl about the box being closed. She was furious. She wanted her mail and wanted it now. I tried to tell her I didn't have her mail. The box was closed. And besides, she hadn't been the box renter. If she would like to submit a change of address card, we could at least have any mail that came in forwarded to her. She screamed at me and swore at me as she left the office. I figured she'd get over it and thought no more of it.

That afternoon, I received a call from the person who used to have the PO box in question, and she told me in no uncertain terms that I would re-open that box and I'd damn well better find her daughter's missing mail because she knew people who would watch for me as I either arrived at the office or left for the day, so I'd better just watch my back. She said it was a long drive from Siletz and anything could happen.

She hadn't given me her phone number and I had to think really fast. I very quietly said I'd try to see what I could do and call her back within the next half hour. I asked what number she could be reached at and what her name was again, without me having to look back through the closed boxes information … just so I could get back to her right away. Thank God she gave it to me, and I called the Postal Inspectors as soon as I hung up. I'm not entirely certain what they said to her when they called her and when they went to see her in person, but I never heard from her again and her daughter never came back. That was a pretty scary day. Even though I knew the inspectors had taken care of the situation, I found myself being very cautious when arriving or leaving for some time to come.

WHEN THINGS GET OUT OF BALANCE

One morning the two Clerks and I were sorting mail when all of a sudden I felt like I was falling. But which direction was I falling? Up? Down? Right? Left? I couldn't tell. I grabbed the letter case for dear life and closed my eyes. I asked Candy to get me a chair and call my husband to come take me to the doctor.

When Perry got me to the doctor and he checked me over, he informed me I had labyrinthitis. I asked him what the heck that was and was it terminal. He laughed, because I looked so terrified, and patted my hand saying it was just an infection in the deep inner ear and I'd need to be flat in bed until it had run its course (about three to four weeks). I wasn't to even try to get up to use the bathroom without help because I'd fall.

A couple of days later, Perry had a fishing trip he had to take out so he called his mom and step-dad to come stay with me. He told them they needed to come real early because I wasn't to get up to use the bathroom without help. They assured him they'd be there early.

I guess early to retired folks isn't as early as we thought because even though Perry helped me to the bathroom before leaving and I didn't drink anything, I finally couldn't hold it any longer when they weren't here by 10:00 a.m.

I tried to get to the bathroom alone. I closed my eyes and slid off the bed onto the floor. I lay flat and felt with my hands to find the edge of the area rug. Keeping my eyes closed, I felt along the edge of the rug, pulling myself along until I got to the end. I swung my arms along the floor until I finally hit the door jam to the bathroom. I then pulled myself through the doorway and felt around until I found the toilet. I pulled myself to my knees and then up the wall until I was standing with my legs by the toilet. I was pretty proud of myself for being so self-sufficient and started to work my way slowly down the wall by placing the fingertips of one hand beneath the palm/wrist of the other. I figured I was almost there. That's when I made my error. I opened my eyes to make sure and that's when I fell. All I could think was, 'Darn! If I'd only kept my eyes closed.' That's where my in-laws found me about half an hour later, and helped me back to bed.

When Perry got home, he came to see how I was and to take me into the bathroom. I tried to get out of bed and couldn't. My right leg had no feeling. They somehow got me into the car and to the Emergency Room in Newport, Oregon. The people on duty at the Emergency Room didn't even check me over. They never took any X-rays. All they did was give me a shot of Demerol in the hip, tell me it was a bruised surface nerve, and to go see my own doctor on Monday.

Well, after 8-1/2 months of that "bruised surface nerve", I couldn't take any more. I have a pretty high pain threshold, but this was even too much for me. I went to see Dr. Fox at the Depoe Bay Clinic and, bless his heart, he sent me right to Dr. Watanabe, a sports medicine specialist in Newport. Between the two of them, they finally got me mobile and most of the pain pretty much gone. The bone chip has been covered over the years with cushioning. I learned that when the doctor tells you not to get out of bed or you'll fall, DON'T GET OUT OF BED!!! Listen to your doctor. They're a lot smarter than we are about these things … trust me.

GOING HOME TO DEPOE BAY

I'd been Postmaster in Siletz a little more than a year when I found out Jack, the Postmaster for Depoe Bay was going to retire. I immediately put in for a lateral transfer due to the fact that I resided in Depoe Bay and the long commute every day was really taking a toll on me with my hip being so bad.

Well, the Postal Service is kinda like the waterfront in a fishing town. If someone finds something out in the morning, you can bet everyone will know about it by evening. A few days after putting in for the lateral transfer, I stopped at the Whistle Stop, which is a Shell service station at the south end of Depoe Bay, to pick up some milk and a newspaper. A new young man that I hadn't seen before was behind the counter, and as I went to pay for my purchases, he asked me if I'd like to sign a petition. I asked what the petition was for, and he said a friend of the Postal Clerk here had left it and that people wanted their local Clerk to get the Postmaster's position and not that ignorant woman from Siletz.

I told him my name was Tanya York and I was that "ignorant" woman from Siletz. I informed him that I lived in Depoe Bay and had for a number of years. I also told him that the "local" Clerk may work here but resided in Newport. I said I was sure the Clerk was very good and a very nice person but he should make very certain of what he was saying to whom in the future because he just might end up with egg on his face.

That poor young man's face turned beet red and he stammered and stuttered all over himself trying to apologize to me. I guess he must have either tossed the petition or given it back because I never saw it again. My lateral transfer came through and I no longer had that long, painful drive every day. My Clerk Bob was a good help during the changeover and I appreciated his help. Boy! Was it ever good to be home.

AN INCREASE IN STAFF

One of the first issues I needed to tackle was the staffing. We definitely needed another PTF Clerk in the office. I discovered the former Postmaster had started the ball rolling to get another Clerk but had decided that since someone new was coming on deck, they should make the decision as to who the new employee should be.

I contacted headquarters and asked to have the position posted and for a copy of the hiring list. I received several transfer requests, including one from a PTF Clerk from Arizona. Her husband was raised in Oregon and had put in for a transfer to the Lincoln City office.

I contacted her Supervisor and asked for a recommendation. He said Lupe was a great employee. She was always punctual, reliable, a hard worker, and got along great with everyone from management on down to the custodian. 'Well now, that's exactly the kind of person I'd like to add to this office,' I thought.

When I met Lupe in person, I was very impressed and hired her to fill the Clerk position. I was so glad I hired her. She definitely was one of the hardest workers I'd ever met and she had the most wonderful way with the customers. They just loved her.

Soon Bob, Lupe, and I became this wonderful team. We worked well together and got a lot accomplished. It was heartwarming to see Bob and Lupe teasing each other like they were brother and sister. I always felt comfortable leaving the office in such capable hands if I had to attend a meeting. I knew the job would get done. Bob had filled in for the former Postmaster and knew how to do the daily books, so that was a big help if I had to attend a meeting. It wasn't long before Lupe had mastered the sorting scheme and was ready to be trained to do the forwards and returns. She caught on really fast and was a real asset to the office.

A CALL FROM HEADQUARTERS

One day I received a call from my MPOO. The first thing you think when headquarters calls is, 'What did I do?' Well, Mr. Bogroff said he needed to send me to Lincoln City on a detail (temporary assignment) and could I think of anyone I'd feel comfortable leaving in charge of my office. The first person I thought of was Candy from Siletz. I knew she'd do a wonderful job. If Bob filled my position, that would leave the office short a Clerk. Yes, Candy was the logical choice.

Mr. Bogroff must have agreed because he had her come to OIC (Officer in Charge) my office. The situation was only supposed to be for a short time, but I'd forgotten that a short time in postal terms isn't necessarily a short time in layman's terms. It turned out to be several months.

It was great being back at the Lincoln City PO. The crew welcomed me back and of course it was great working with everyone again.

Doug the Postmaster and his wife Nina had lost a baby, and when they became pregnant again, they were very cautious and followed all the doctor's orders to the letter. When their precious little Rebecca made her debut, it was a joyous occasion. I was blown away when they approached me and asked me if I'd be Rebecca's Godmother. What an honor to bestow on someone. Of course I accepted. Rebecca's first few months were a struggle and she had to be rushed to the hospital on several occasions. You'd sure never know now that she'd ever had a problem. She's such a beautiful child and such a blessing.

I settled back into the "family" in the Lincoln City office very quickly and was both excited to have this opportunity and anxious for the "short" time to pass so I could get back to my own office. Candy, Bob, Lupe, and the HCR (Highway

Contract Route) Carrier David did a great job in my absence and I really appreciated them.

BE CAREFUL WHAT YOU SAY IN A SMALL TOWN

I was back at my office. My crew and I were really kicking butt getting the mail out in a timely manner, and the customers all seemed to be happy as a lark. Life was good ... busy, but good.

April rolled around, and as the 15th got closer, customers got grumpier. The mail volume got heavier, but we were doing pretty good at keeping up. April 15th was really busy, as it always is. We had a long line at 5:00 p.m., but not as busy as I had anticipated. We got all the customers taken care of, closed the window line, and got the mail dispatch out on time.

That evening I received a phone call at home stating there was something I should know. The caller stated they'd overheard my Clerk telling customers that if they'd drop their tax envelopes in the outside mail drop, the Clerk would make sure to cancel them with the 15th's date upon arriving at the PO the next morning. The caller said they knew my standard of ethics and also knew I would definitely not approve of such actions. I thanked him (still don't know who the caller was to this day) and made my plans to arrive extra early the next morning.

Upon my arrival at the office, I immediately pulled all the mail from all of the inside and outside mail drops and hand-cancelled them with the proper date. I then called headquarters, which I was required to do, and related what had happened. When asked if the Clerk was scheduled to work that day, I said, "Yes," and related the scheduled work hours.

Headquarters called later and asked to speak with the Clerk involved. Headquarters told me later that the Clerk had been told it was a blessing I was the Postmaster and had gone to bat for them because their job wouldn't have been if not for that fact. Needless to say, I never had ANY problems of that nature again! Just goes to show ... be careful of what you say and who's within earshot ... in a small town.

AN OLD MOTHER HEN WITH HER CHICKS

You know, over the years I've learned to just go with the flow and not let too much get under my skin, but every now and then I have my moments. Like with my Clerks. You can get in my face about something all you want to, but don't even think I'm going to stand by and see one of my Clerks being verbally abused or have a customer treat one of them shabbily.

I had never known Lupe to be upset by a customer. Then I started noticing that every time this one business owner came in and Lupe had to wait on him, she was visibly nervous. One day after he'd been in, I asked her if there was a problem. She said he always acted like he thought she was stupid and it made her very afraid she'd make a mistake.

From that time on, if that customer came into the office and Lupe was on the window line, I'd help him or have one of the other Clerks take over the window if I didn't have my till in. I'd make some excuse to pull her off the window and have her do another project. Bless her heart. She would never have complained and would have kept feeling uncomfortable. That just goes to show who the true professional of the two was.

Remember, all you people in management, whether you work in the Postal Service or for a service station, be aware of your people who work for you. Don't you browbeat them and don't ever stand for letting someone else browbeat them. That's why we're in management .. because the buck stops with us. Our employees shouldn't have to deal with rude, obnoxious, unreasonable customers. That's our job! If you want loyalty from your crew, be there to back them.

AND IT'S INTO THE COMPUTER AGE

Boy! The older I get, the faster time seems to pass me by. Seems like I just get one way of doing business figured out and we head off in another direction. First it was stamps, then meter strips for postage, and now it's the computer systems on the window line.

Well, as busy as the Depoe Bay office is, I want those IRTs for my office. I decided that if I made a pest out of myself and called every week asking for them, they'd get tired of my calling and give in and give me the IRTs.

It took almost two years of calling every week, but it finally paid off. The last time I called, I was told I'd be getting my computers that next week when they'd be down in my area, so please don't call.

When they brought me only one PVI (Post Validating Imprinter) but promised the other one would be sent right down, I guess upon arrival back in Portland the office gal was instructed to send me the PVI ASAP or I'd call every day until I got it. I guess that old adage about the squeaky wheel getting the oil is true. Anyway, we got our computer system. My Clerks got trained and we were able to offer much better service to our customers at the counter.

I'm pretty easygoing, but if I'm convinced we need something for our office that will allow better service to our customers, watch out, because I'll dig my heels in and not budge until we get it. At the same time, I don't ask for something unless it's really important and I feel it will help the office in meeting our office budget commitment. My goal is to always give my customers the very best service we can give them, and at the same time, do the very best job possible in meeting the office budget that headquarters has set forth for us.

ONE'S A GOING AND ONE'S A COMING

I was really concerned when Bob said he was going to retire after 22 years working for the Postal Service. I sure hoped and prayed I'd be able to fill the position relatively easy. I couldn't post the position until Bob officially was retired. In the meantime, I'd have to borrow a Clerk from another office. We'd muddle through.

Lupe and I had one of Bob's friends help us put on a big retirement party for Bob when his big day finally came to be a reality. It was a huge success and we were able to send him into that magical world of retirement with a bang.

One day I received a call from Roberta Polly, the Supervisor of the Lincoln City PO. She wanted to ask me if I'd consider hiring her as my needed PTF Clerk. I asked her if she was serious and if she had thought this through. She assured me she and her husband had talked it all through and he only wanted her to be happy where she worked. She said she'd be willing to take the pay cut and the, very often, six days a week to have the opportunity to work for me again.

Well, I sure didn't have to think to know what my answer was. I was so honored that she felt so strongly about working with me. Here was this gal who I had helped train years ago as a PTF. I'd watched her grow and develop her management skills until she'd finally been promoted to Supervisor. Now here she was asking me to let her come work for me again and was willing to step down several grade levels to do so. Watch out world. Now, with Roberta and Lupe, I'd have the "Dream Team". We could move mountains.

Those two girls worked so well together. I never, in all the time they worked for me, ever heard a mean or harsh word from either one. What a load off my shoulders to have my whole crew, including my HCR Carrier, like and respect each other.

They always were there for me and for each other to do whatever it took to make the team a success. What more could a Postmaster ask for?

Talk about being committed to their job. Lupe's poor little hands would hurt her so bad sometimes, but pain or not, she was there giving it 150 percent. And without saying a word, on the days when Lupe's pain was worse than others, Roberta dug down within herself and somehow managed to put forth that extra effort that helped us pull through. Now that's teamwork at its finest, and I was the chosen one who was blessed enough to have them.

OKAY GUYS, TAKE IT OUTSIDE

You think you know your customers pretty good when you're in a small town. After all, they aren't just your customers, they're neighbors, people you volunteer at functions with and sit next to at a community potluck.

I really thought I knew these two "pillars of the community" who served our community in such an outstanding way. They were always there to help with an event in any way they could. I guess even big-hearted guys have their days now and then.

I was in my office one afternoon doing some bookkeeping and computer work when I heard voices getting louder and louder. At first I thought someone was yelling at my Clerk, and we know how that goes over with me. I poked my head out the door and around the corner by the window line. It was at this point that I discovered what the source of vocalizing was. There they stood, face to face, poking each other in the chests with their fingers and talking in a more than slightly raised voice to each other.

Now, being the nice, quiet, refined lady that I am (not), I immediately went and opened the door from my office to the window lobby and invited them into the sanctity of my inner office. I softly closed the door, turned to them and said, "How dare you come into my Post Office and act this way. I bend over backwards for all my customers and this is how you show respect? By coming in here and acting like a couple of snot-nosed juveniles who haven't the maturity yet to be able to control themselves? If you guys have a problem with each other, don't go bringing it into the Post Office. I had more confidence than this in both of you. In the future, if you have a problem, take it to one of your own front yards, but never, ever bring something of this kind into my Post Office again. This is the end of it as far as I'm concerned and I'll not bring it up again. I hope neither of you do. Now go behave like the adults

I know you to be." They sheepishly left and from that day on were perfect examples of the gentlemen I'd always known them to be.

Okay Guys, Take it Outside

A LESSON IN BREAD-MAKING

Over the years, I've been very blessed to have met so many really great people while in the employ of the United States Postal Service. In thinking back to all of those great people who touched my life, I feel very humble to have them in my life. If I were to talk about even a small portion of them, I'd have to write a book as big as the thickest dictionary ever printed.

There is one lady who keeps jumping into my thoughts, and I thought I'd like to share a little experience we had. Nancy Cox and her husband Dr. Jay Cox came into the Post Office to rent a PO box, and immediately they touched my heart with their gentle smiles and quick sense of humor. As time went on and I had the opportunity to visit with them (mostly with Nancy), I found that this sweet, gentle woman was so genuine and sincere. There wasn't a single unkind thing that I ever heard come out of her mouth.

One day, as we talked and I told her about how much I enjoyed being a mom and what fun I had baking bread with my children, she made the comment that she'd love to learn how to bake bread. I invited her to come to my house and we'd have a bread baking lesson.

We set a date, and when the day came, it was kind of drizzly outside. I got up early that morning and put a big pot of homemade vegetable beef soup on to cook. Nancy arrived and commented on the wonderful smell of, as she put it, something really mouth-watering. I said it was our lunch cooking. The fresh yeast rolls should be done about 12:30 or 1:00 p.m. and we'd "break bread" together to celebrate our bread baking lesson.

We set about mixing our separate batches of bread side by side there in my kitchen while we chatted like dear old friends.

Nancy was a great student, and her bread turned out as mouth watering as any I'd ever turned out in my years of baking bread.

We had our lunch of homemade soup, fresh baked bread, and ice cold milk. I guess I've probably eaten as wonderful a meal in my life, but I certainly can't remember when. I think it had as much to do with the company as the food.

As our time together came to an end that day and Nancy headed for home, I knew this day would live in my special storehouse of memories for the rest of my life. Many times since that day we have talked about our great time together and our very special bread baking lesson. She now bakes bread sometimes for Jay and he loves it.

BIG CHANGES IN THE HCR ROUTE

One of my big goals when I became Postmaster in Depoe Bay was to get street delivery. I was so concerned about my customers having to cross busy Highway 101 twice just to come to get their mail. I was especially concerned about the folks living in Little Whale Cove. It's a gated community at the south of Depoe Bay and a large percentage of the people who reside there are senior citizens. The highway is extremely busy in that area and several of my customers had come in saying they had nearly gotten hit by a vehicle going too fast.

I began by doing my homework so when I approached headquarters with my request I'd have all my ducks in a row. I told my husband that I'd become a streetwalker because I had to literally walk every darn street in this town and write down every address to be able to present my case favorably. It got to the point that someone would come in and tell me their address and I'd say, "Oh, yeah. The blue house on the corner of ---," or, "Yes. The yellow house next to the gray one." I could close my eyes and put a house with nearly any address you might fling at me.

I was able to convince headquarters this move was for the safety of our customers and they gave me the go-ahead to start the project. It was decided we'd put 18 NDCBUs in, starting with everything south of the Depoe Bay bridge, and then another 17 NDCBUs in at Little Whale Cove. When the announcement was made to the customers, why you'd have thought I'd just informed them that they were going to be taken out at dawn and be shot. They didn't want any part of any old Neighborhood Delivery, Collection, Box Units in their midst.

It took a lot of patience and gentle convincing to get the customers to accept this move into the future, but they finally accepted it. It's so funny because those people who complained the loudest were the ones who came back later saying how great they were and how they wished it could have been done a long time ago. When the time rolled around to get NDCBUs in Little Whale Cove, I'd talked with my Clerks and the HCR Carrier and we planned a big question and answer session at the hall in Little Whale Cove. The Carrier and I had made a list of all the addresses and I'd gotten boxes with small sections for the keys. We passed out keys to nearly all of the residents that night and ended up saving ourselves a lot of time on the window line because we didn't have to utilize our time running back and forth getting keys for people.

David was probably one of the absolute best Carriers I've ever come across. He was able to grow with the route and hired his two adult daughters to help on the route. When David started on the route, he had 247 deliveries. By the time we'd finished putting everything from south of the bridge all the way to and including Little Whale Cove, the route had grown to more than 860 deliveries.

David does an outstanding job on the route. The customers love him. He not only delivers their mail, but he and his wife Bobbi go out of their way to help some of the elderly people on his route by taking them to the store, to the doctor, etc. I have even known David to load up his lawnmower and go mow yards for those who can't do it themselves. Now that's a Carrier who really cares about the people on his route. Sure am glad he's part of our team. I did a good job the day I recommended he be hired. I'm thankful headquarters listened. He's a real asset to the Postal Service.

HEY! I DIDN'T ORDER AN INDOOR POOL!

We may not have many forest fires here on the central Oregon coast and it doesn't snow very often, but one thing we do have an abundance of is rain. If you have an aversion to rain, don't think of moving to our area. After all, it's because of the rain we have all the beautiful green trees, lovely flowers, and some of the most gorgeous rainbows a person has ever laid their eyes on. Mother Nature sometimes is overly generous in the rain she sends, but we "webfoots" are used to it and usually pay it no mind. I say usually because sometimes even we get exasperated when there seems to be no end in sight for the rain.

We were experiencing such a wet spell that had lasted for longer than usual. The Depoe Bay PO is built on flat ground where the building sits, but out back the ground slants upward at a very steep angle to Williams Street. Williams Street runs north and south from Lane Street to Collins Street. East of Williams Street, the ground again angles quite steeply up the mountain. There had been a lot of building done all along the east side of Williams Street -- to the top of the mountain in some places -- so an awful lot of trees and shrubs had been removed. All of those days accumulation of heavy rainfall had to eventually go someplace.

The morning had gone along pretty well until one of the Clerks went into the loading vestibule to retrieve the cart for parcel sorting. She noticed some water seeping in from the back door. By the time I, the other Clerk, and the HCR Carrier had gone to help, we had a small wall of water pouring through the back doorway.

The Carrier used the large, rubber backed rug to hold back as much water as possible. The rest of us scrambled to get any of the mail sitting on the floor onto higher, dryer areas. Thanks to quick action on everyone's part, not one piece of mail or any packages got even damp.

As soon as the mail was secured, I called the City to see if they had a wet/dry vacuum, then called my husband to bring down our wet/dry vacuum. I called headquarters to let them know what had happened and that no mail had been damaged and the water was being vacuumed up with two large wet/dry vacuums.

I'd locked the front doors and posted a notice explaining the situation. In a little over an hour, we had all of the water gone, the floors mopped with bleach water, and the lower three to four inches of the wall where the water had gotten was washed with bleach water.

The doors were once again opened and it was business as usual (well, almost usual). We were even able to get the mail up on time, thanks to the light volume that day. Those of us who were there will always remember when we almost had an indoor pool at the Depoe Bay PO.

I'M SORRY YOU'RE LOST

Just when you think you've heard them all, some darn fool has to come along and prove you wrong. Being a vacationer's dream area, we are quite used to receiving mail addressed to a street address rather than a PO box, so when mail started to show up with a street address, it was not out of the ordinary … except for one small item. We have no NE 13th Street in Depoe Bay.

I began calling other nearby Post Offices to see if they had such an address. The only one who did was Lincoln City, but that address was showing as a vacant address. The Supervisor was going to have the Carrier physically check to be sure it was, in fact, vacant, and would call me upon his return to the office. When she called me later that day, she informed me the property was vacant and showed absolutely no signs of anyone being there.

I called the Post Office in Nebraska and told the Postmaster to stop forwarding mail for that person as we had no such address out of our Post Office and that in checking, I'd found it was not a good forward for any of the outlying offices. I returned the pieces that had already entered the mail stream as "No such address". After a few days, we stopped receiving any more mail and I thought no more about it.

Well, about three months later, this man comes barreling into my Post Office ready to rip my head off and spit in the hole. He was ranting and raving about us having sent his mail back as undeliverable because we didn't happen to recognize the address. He went on and on about how stupid and incompetent we were and how he had connections and he'd see to it we were all fired.

I held up my hand and quietly (I was too angry to speak in a regular tone of voice) told him to calm down for a minute and

I'd try to help him. I told him I couldn't fix a problem until I knew exactly what the problem was, what the origin was, and then we could go about trying to fix it. He started to raise his voice again, and I said, "Stop talking to me in that raised voice or this conversation is over. I'm trying to help you if you'll let me. I will not tolerate being yelled at or sworn at. Now, let's try to figure out what has happened."

It seems that he had purchased a home in Lincoln City a few years ago in the anticipation of retiring there. When he retired and decided to move, he had simply turned in a change of address form and had put down Depoe Bay as the town instead of Lincoln City. He couldn't see what the big deal was. These towns along the coast weren't very big, so he couldn't see why we couldn't just change his order and deliver his mail.

I informed him I'd checked with Lincoln City and found out that piece of property had been vacant and overgrown for some time and no one had contacted the Post Office to let them know someone was moving in. I also reminded him that it had been over three months since I'd returned his mail. Why did it take him so long to discover the problem? He told me that it was really none of my business, but he'd decided to do a little traveling before moving in.

I'd been sitting there across the desk from him, listening and taking notes, for quite awhile, and it seemed he had his mind made up that we were the "stupid enemy" and that was that. I lay my pen down, stood up, and said to him, "Sir, I'm very sorry for your problem. I tried, I really did, to get your problem fixed, but, sir, if you don't know where you live, how do you expect me to know where you live?"

He looked at me with the strangest look on his face for a minute. Then all of a sudden he must have realized just how silly he had been sounding because he lowered his head, softly (I could barely hear him) said he was sorry, and left. I sure hope he finally found out where he lived. I'd hate to have him still wandering around trying to find himself.

VOLUNTEERING IN DEPOE BAY

As anyone who lives in a small town can tell you, volunteering becomes a very big part of your life. Nowhere is this more evident than in this small fishing/tourist town of Depoe Bay. You don't just volunteer for one event. You volunteer for many different events throughout the year (and we have LOTS of them).

Over the years, I've enjoyed helping with many different ones, but the two nearest and dearest to my heart are the annual Fleet of Flowers on Memorial Day and the Indian Style Salmon Bake the third Saturday of September every year.

I was blessed enough to be in charge of the most wonderful group of volunteers for the Fleet of Flowers for many years. This function is one of the most touching you will ever experience. If you have never been to Depoe Bay for this heart-touching event, please make it a point to come. I can guarantee it will change your life forever.

Each year, a huge group of volunteers spend an entire week making thousands of wreaths. On Memorial Day, all of the wreaths that have been made are divided amongst the charter boats, and the captains and crew decorate the boats with them. At 11:00 a.m., there is a beautiful ceremony by the Coast Guard Station. After the ceremony, people board the boats and all of the boats leave the harbor single file and proceed to the buoy where the boats form a huge circle. Then the Coast Guard helicopter flies over and drops a large ceremonial wreath in the center of the circle of boats. At that point, everyone on the boats places all of the wreaths upon the waters. The ocean becomes this huge blanket of flowers. I've done this for over twelve years and I always feel humbled by the touching way this is done.

In September every year, we have the Salmon Bake. Again … all done by volunteers who believe in giving back. Each year we serve a couple of thousand meals.

The salmon is cooked on sticks over this huge fire pit Indian style. Talk about mouthwatering. It's like no fish you've ever been blessed enough to put into your mouth. I love working the Indian Style Salmon Bake. I plan to still be working it when I'm ninety years old. I'm sure they can find something for me to do.

Then there's the Wooden Boat Show, Crab Feed, community potlucks, Neighborhood Watch, Kid's Zone, Rowing Club. Well, I could go on for awhile. You get the picture. There's plenty to volunteer for.

Plus, the bonus is … you meet the nicest people. Why, I even met this one guy Jim King who grew up in the same town my mom grew up in, Blackduck, Minnesota. Now how many people in Oregon have a clue where Blackduck, Minnesota is? Yet here I am, cutting boughs for the Fleet of Flowers one year, and I get to visiting with some of the other people and find out that Jim was from my mom's hometown. He and his wife Jean can be found at nearly every event helping.

CAPTURE HISTORY BEFORE IT'S GONE

Every town and city, no matter the size, has a virtual gold mine of that town's history if we will only avail ourselves of it. I'm talking about the "old timers" from the area who are full of stories by the bucketful. If we seek these local treasures out and get them to talking about the old days, we can find ourselves transported into another time full of people and places we'd never even imagined.

I've been blessed to have had some of these "treasures" cross my life's path, and I can tell you .. it's a wonder to behold when you are amongst those chosen to be honored with tales from the past.

The first such treasure that comes to mind is Fred Robison here in Depoe Bay. Fred's family has lived in the area almost since time began. (Well, maybe not quite that long.) But they have been around for a very long time. Fred is a quiet, gentle guy who possesses all the charm and gentlemanly manners of a bygone era.

On the occasions when you are fortunate enough to be present at one of his "remember when" stories, I can assure you that you will be spellbound. Fred is one of the best storytellers. He can transport you back and make you feel you were there and a part of the whole thing. Fred and his wife Betty, a tiny elegant lady with a heart of purest gold, live in a home here in Depoe Bay that sits above the harbor and overlooks the ocean. They are true treasures of our community. Plus, they make the best darn hot dogs I've ever tasted!!

Another treasure I've been blessed with in my life is Chief Chewescla, better known as William (Bill) Depoe, the Chief of the Siletz Indians. Bill is the great-grandson of Chief Depoe. The town of Depoe Bay is named after him.

I met Bill and his beautiful wife Norma several years ago and they have become very dear friends. We've kept in touch and get together for dinner every year when they come for the Fleet of Flowers. Bill is a quiet, proud man who stands straight and tall and has the kindest, gentlest manner about him. I can remember sitting in our living room listening to him tell of his father, grandfather, and great-grandfather. We all listened as this very humble man told story after story about the hardships his ancestors went through. You could see the pain in his eyes as he told his stories, yet he holds no resentment and is a very loving, gentle man.

As you look around your own town or city, don't overlook those treasures that can be found in your own backyard. The riches you'll reap will bless your lives forever. I know I'm richer for having "treasures" in my life.

THERE'S CHANGES TAKING PLACE

Lupe decided to join the ranks of the retired after more than 22 years of being in the "postal family". She'll be sorely missed. What will I do without my "Dream Team"?

Lupe will do great though. She touched our lives and made them richer. Now it's time for her to enrich the lives of all those people waiting to meet her. She'll come into their lives like a whirlwind, without warning. Before they know it, that big smile and bubbly personality will have them eating out of her hand. I've seen people come into the Post Office with a chip on their shoulder and leave laughing after Lupe waited on them. I'm lucky to have had the opportunity to work with Lupe. Oh, my! How will I ever replace her?

As I sat at my desk one afternoon trying to catch up, a knock came on my office door. When I answered the knock, there stood a guy with dark, curly hair asking if I had time to talk. I said, "Sure," and invited him into the office.

He said his name was Doug and his fiancée had just been promoted to Postmaster in Newport, Oregon. Since I was looking for a Clerk, would I consider taking him as a transfer? We talked for awhile, and I said I thought it would work fine, but I had to contact his Supervisor first about it.

I called his Supervisor and asked for his OPF (Official Personnel File). After going through his files, I talked with Doug and asked if he was ready to come join our crew. He was more than ready. David, the HCR Carrier, was glad too because he'd have another guy in the office instead of being surrounded by girl people all the time.

I used to get tickled at Doug and David. They loved to spar with each other verbally. They'd get started, and then pretty soon you'd see one of them grin and that twinkle in their eyes.

Sometimes I felt like a den mother with those two. They really got along well. They were both just little boys in grown-up britches that had to tease.

REMEMBER ME ... I'LL REMEMBER YOU

Well now, just how do I go about closing this chapter of my life? The day has finally come for me to step aside, after more than twenty years, and let someone else take the torch and keep it burning. I hope I've been able to touch your lives as memorably as you've touched mine. It's been a grand journey with you.

There have been a few bumps in the road and even some potholes now and again. There were happy times, sad times, scary times, bizarre times, stressful times, and any other kind of times you can think of, but we were always there, in it together. I hope you'll remember me from time to time, for I can guarantee you I'll remember you ... forever!

IT'S A PARTY

Thanks to my husband Perry and my wonderful crew, I'm leaving my postal service career the same as I started it, with Bill Layton at the helm. I am so honored that the same Postmaster who brought me into the postal family fold will be Master of Ceremonies at my retirement party. Having Bill and Sally Layton come all this way to see me off as I start out on my journey into the life of retirement is the ultimate thrill. I can't imagine any better send-off.

As I looked around the room at my retirement party, I was reminded of how blessed I really am. So many Postmasters, Supervisors, Clerks, and Carriers were there. Some had come from up the road, and some had come from many miles away. And there were my customers (my friends), whose sweet faces smiled back at me from all around. All had come to wish me well (or maybe it was to make sure I left) and I was touched to the bottom of my heart. And then there was my wonderfully loving family. They had always been there in my corner throughout the years. Now here they were again, to share in my joy of retirement. God surely must love me a lot to have let me enjoy such a terrific adventure down life's road with all of you.

If I have ever said or done anything to hurt any of you, I apologize. If any of you have said or done anything to hurt me, I apologize for giving you reason to do so. You have blessed my life. May yours be blessed as well.

* * *